A Timeline of the
CALIFORNIA GOLD RUSH

Kerri O'Donnell

The Rosen Publishing Group's
PowerKids Press™
New York

Published in 2009 by The Rosen Publishing Group, Inc.
29 East 21st Street, New York, NY 10010

Book Design: Haley W. Harasymiw

Photo Credits: Cover, pp. 5, 10, 11, 12, 13, 20, 22, 25, 26 © Hulton Archive/Getty Images; cover, pp. 2–32 (gold border) © bonsai/Shutterstock; p. 4 © Mark Kauffman/Time & Life Pictures/Getty Images; p. 6 http://en.wikipedia.org/wiki/Image:JohannAugustSutter2.jpg; p. 7 http://en.wikipedia.org/wiki/Image: James_Marshall2.jpg; p. 8 (oregon trail map) http://en.wikipedia.org/wiki/Image:Oregontrail_1907.jpg; p. 9 © The Bridgeman Art Library/Getty Images; pp. 14, 17 © California State Library; p. 19 http://en.wikipedia.org/wiki/Image:SanFranciscoharbor1851c_sharp.jpg; pp. 28–29 © Timothy Hearsum/ The Image Bank/Getty Images; p. 30 © Nina B./Shutterstock.

Library of Congress Cataloging-in-Publication Data

O'Donnell, Kerri, 1972-
  A timeline of the California Gold Rush / Kerri O'Donnell.
     p. cm. - (Real life readers)
  Includes index.
  ISBN 978-1-4358-2989-3 (lib. bdg.)
  ISBN: 978-1-4358-0161-5 (paperback)
  6-pack ISBN: 978-1-4358-0162-2
  1. California-Gold discoveries—Juvenile literature. 2. Gold mines and mining—California—History—19th century—Juvenile literature. 3. California—History—1846–1850—Juvenile literature. I. Title.
  F865.O364 2009
  979.4'04-dc22

                              2008041651

Manufactured in the United States of America

Contents

A Golden Discovery

On January 24, 1848, a man named James Marshall made one of the most important discoveries in U.S. history. That morning, while overseeing the construction of a sawmill in central California, he found something that would change the country forever—gold!

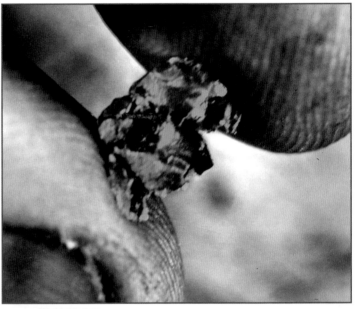

This is a photo of the gold nugget James Marshall found in 1848. Today, the gold nugget is kept in the Smithsonian Institution.

Marshall worked for John Sutter, a Swiss businessman who had settled in California's northern Central Valley. Sutter built a place he called "Sutter's Fort" on the land near where the American and Sacramento Rivers come together. Sutter's Fort served as headquarters

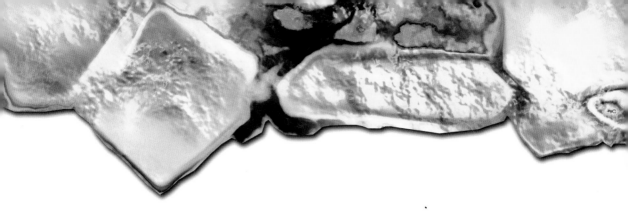

for Sutter's many businesses, including a sawmill that he hoped would supply settlers in the area with lumber.

The sawmill—known as Sutter's Mill—was being built at the place that is today the town of Coloma, which was about 48 miles (77 km) from Sutter's Fort on the southern part of the American River. It was in this river that Marshall saw that fateful flash of gold.

Sutter's Mill, California, 1848

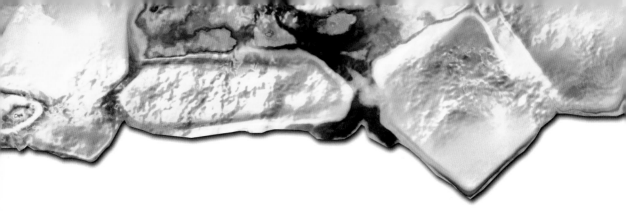

Sutter tried to keep Marshall's discovery secret. He knew that once the news spread, his land would be overrun by hopeful miners in search of gold. That would delay the opening of his sawmill.

The secret soon got out, though, and spread quickly throughout California. Sutter's workers left their jobs to dig for gold along the American River and its **tributaries**. By March 1848, the news reached San Francisco, along with a sample of gold flakes that was publicly

John Sutter

Surprisingly, John Sutter didn't profit from the gold rush. He died a poor man in 1880.

displayed. "Gold fever" had begun, and large numbers of **prospectors** began to arrive in the area.

It wasn't long before the news spread across the United States, over the Atlantic Ocean to Europe, south into Mexico and South America, and west across the Pacific Ocean to Asia. Marshall's discovery caused a huge **migration** that changed California—and the United States—forever.

James Marshall

1839—John Sutter arrives in California. Mexico's governor gives Sutter a land grant for 48,000 acres.

July 1845—James Marshall arrives at Sutter's Fort after traveling by wagon train from Oregon.

August 1847— Sutter hires Marshall to build a sawmill.

September 1847— Marshall and his crew begin building Sutter's Mill.

January 24, 1848— Marshall discovers gold near Sutter's Mill.

The United States Takes California

In the mid-1840s, California wasn't part of the United States. It was part of Mexico, which had been established as a republic in 1821 when people living in Mexico overthrew Spanish rule.

While under Spanish rule, California was far away from the Spanish colonial leaders in central Mexico. This made it hard to supply California with the goods it needed to attract new settlers. Once Mexico declared its freedom from Spain, California's ports were opened to other countries for trade, and the region flourished.

By the 1840s, people from the eastern United States had begun to travel west along **transcontinental** trails to start new lives on the **frontier**. These pioneers packed up whatever belongings they could fit into their wagons, leaving the lives they knew behind. A small number made it as far as California.

The Oregon Trail was perhaps the most important transcontinental route established by the pioneers in the years leading up to the gold rush. It was also the longest trail, covering about 2,000 miles (3,200 km).

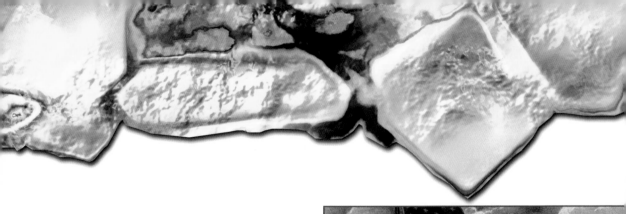

By 1845, California was the last large colonial **outpost** still owned by Mexico. Pioneers from the eastern United States who had settled there didn't want to give up their U.S. citizenship, and many urged the United States to **annex** California. At that time, many U.S. citizens thought the United States had the right to own all the land from the Atlantic Ocean in the east to the Pacific Ocean in the west. Conflicts between the United States and Mexico grew, and war with Mexico over the California territory seemed unavoidable.

This image shows American troops during the Battle of Monterrey, an important battle during the Mexican-American War.

On May 13, 1846, the United States declared war on Mexico. Though the Mexican-American War lasted almost 2 years, the United States' **occupation** of California during this time was largely uncontested. When the war ended on February 2, 1848—just days after James Marshall found gold in California—the United States had won. California officially belonged to the United States.

1860 map of the Mexican-American War

1821—Mexico overthrows Spain's colonial government and becomes a republic.

May 13, 1846—The United States declares war on Mexico, beginning the Mexican-American War.

1840s—Groups of pioneers from the eastern United States travel west, some settling in California.

February 2, 1848—The United States wins the Mexican-American War.

11

Off to the Golden Land

Settlers already in California began to arrive in the goldfields of central California in the spring of 1848. The first gold seekers to arrive from outside of California were from other countries, not the United States. Transcontinental railroads and **telegraph** lines had not yet been established, so the news spread slowly across the country. Travel by land was very slow. Most news traveled by ship, and even that was slow.

Ships first had to sail down the Pacific coast, around South America, then north up the Atlantic coast of South America to the eastern United States. This could take 6 months! Ships traveling to Asia or South America could make the trip more quickly. As a result, gold seekers from other countries began to arrive in California before people in the eastern United States had even heard that gold had been discovered.

James Polk

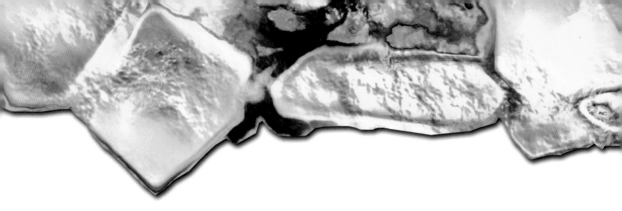

When news finally reached the eastern United States, many didn't believe it. Then, on December 5, 1848—almost a year after James Marshall first found gold—President James Polk announced to Congress that the stories were indeed true.

This image, likely created in early 1848, shows workers panning for gold.

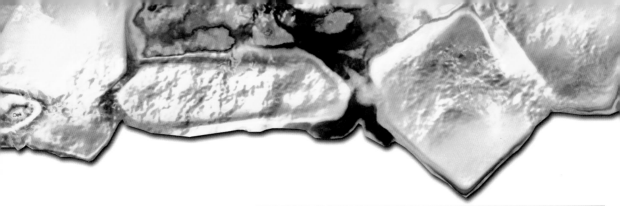

Within days of President Polk's statement, gold fever swept through the eastern United States. About 1,400 ships soon set sail from the eastern United States and Canada, bound for California.

The trip down the Atlantic coast, around the tip of South America, and up the Pacific coast to California covered about 20,000 miles (32,000 km). A shorter

This 1849 map shows the different water routes from the eastern United States to California. The left side of the map shows the western United States. California's gold region is shown in yellow.

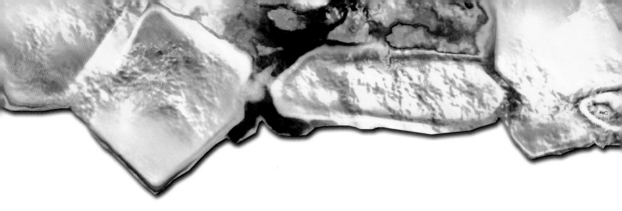

course combined water and land routes. People sailed south to the **Isthmus** of Panama, a strip of land about 50 miles (80 km) wide that connects North and South America. They traveled by foot across the isthmus, and then boarded another ship that took them north to California.

Both routes were dangerous. For those traveling around South America, rough waters and strong winds could send ships off course toward Antarctica. Many travelers using the sea-land route caught illnesses carried by mosquitoes when crossing through Panama's jungle. Some people died from these illnesses.

March 15, 1848—The first printed story about Marshall's discovery of gold appears in a San Francisco newspaper.

July 1848—California's military governor tours California to confirm that there is gold in the region.

December 5, 1848—President James Polk announces to Congress that gold was found in Califorina.

May 1848—The first large group of gold miners arrive at Sutter's Fort.

August 1848—*New York Herald* is the first major East Coast newspaper to report on gold in California.

February 1849—The first ship from the East Coast carrying miners arrives in San Francisco Bay.

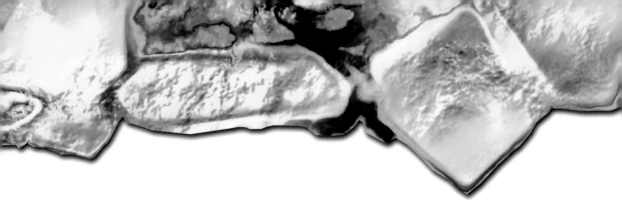

Some hopeful gold seekers traveled across the country by land, earning the nickname "overlanders." The overlanders traveled on the trails previous pioneers had mapped out before the gold rush. They usually joined other travelers to make the long journey with their belongings loaded into wagons and on the backs of their animals.

Most overlanders took the Oregon Trail. It began in Independence, Missouri, and crossed over the plains, through the Rocky Mountains, and over deserts to the Pacific Northwest. Around

Dangers of the Journey to California

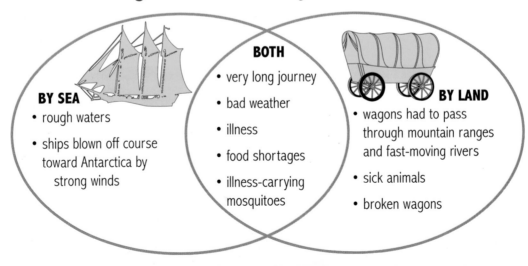

BY SEA
- rough waters
- ships blown off course toward Antarctica by strong winds

BOTH
- very long journey
- bad weather
- illness
- food shortages
- illness-carrying mosquitoes

BY LAND
- wagons had to pass through mountain ranges and fast-moving rivers
- sick animals
- broken wagons

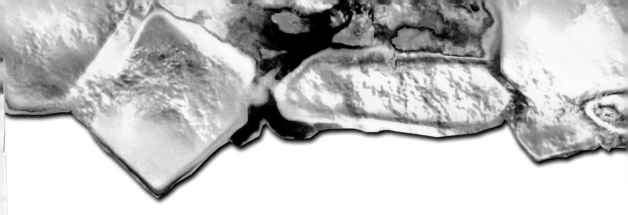

Though some miners did become rich, most prospectors found that their dreams of gold didn't match the truth of life in the mining camps. A usual day began at sunrise with a breakfast of coffee and biscuits, followed by an entire day of digging and "panning" for gold. It was a slow process. The miner would dig the dirt, put it in a pan with water, then swirl the mixture around to slowly wash the dirt over the pan's edge. Any gold in the dirt would stay in the pan since it was heavier. If there was any gold at all, it was usually a small amount and not worth much.

Weeks or even months could pass before miners found any gold. Many had to take other jobs just to make a living. Meanwhile, merchants who had settled in the mining camps often charged the miners high prices for goods such as food, clothes, and tools. The miners had no choice but to buy the expensive goods.

By 1850, California had a large enough population to become a state. On September 9, 1850, California became the thirty-first state. The population continued to grow, and the crime rate grew along with it. Because California had grown so quickly, no official justice system or police force had yet been established to

This drawing, made around 1849, shows a California gold miner and his bag of gold. Note that he is well armed and seems prepared for any bandit who might try to steal his gold.

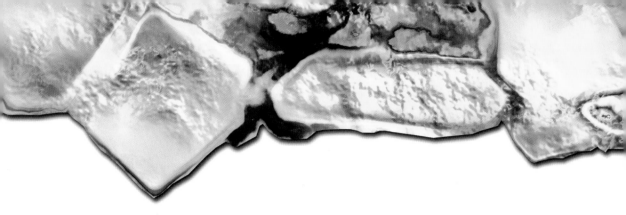

punish people who broke the law. Bandits roamed the region, often attacking miners and stealing their possessions.

The only recognized "law" at the time was called the "miner's code," which consisted of agreements between miners rather than official laws. The miner's code listed the miners' rights and responsibilities as part of the mining community. When these "laws" were broken, other miners took the law into their own hands, and the punishments were often severe. There were no judges or juries to hear people's cases. If a group of miners found a person guilty, he could be put to death without a trial.

May 1849—The first overlanders begin their journey west to California.

September 9, 1850—California becomes the thirty-first state in the United States.

1850—San Francisco grows to a city of 25,000 people; California's population grows to 100,000 people.

Discrimination in the Mines

After **immigrants** from around the world began arriving in California, mining towns and cities such as San Francisco became filled with people of different nationalities, cultures, and religions. California became home to large groups of Mexican, Latin American, and Chinese immigrants, along with many other immigrants who came to find gold and a better life. Instead, many of them found hardship and **discrimination**.

White American miners distrusted the immigrants because they didn't understand the immigrants' ways of life. Immigrant miners were sometimes wrongly accused of crimes they hadn't committed. In April 1850, a law was passed that required every immigrant miner to pay $20 a month for a mining permit. This law, called the Foreign Miners Tax, only made the situation between the American and immigrant miners worse.

This photo, taken around 1855, shows Chinese miners digging and panning for gold. By 1852, more than 20,000 Chinese immigrants are believed to have arrived in San Francisco.

The Foreign Miners Tax was **repealed** in March 1851, only to be followed in 1852 with another tax that required immigrant miners to pay $3 per month. This unfair tax—along with the constant discrimination they faced—forced many immigrants to return to their home countries, or leave the mines to work on farms.

Most African American miners also faced discrimination during the gold rush.

By 1852, gold was becoming harder to find in California. Many American miners blamed immigrants for this, and some formed groups that attacked immigrants and stole their belongings. Those most often targeted were Chinese and Latin American miners. Native Americans, who had lived in California much longer than the Americans and immigrants, were frequently attacked and forced off their lands.

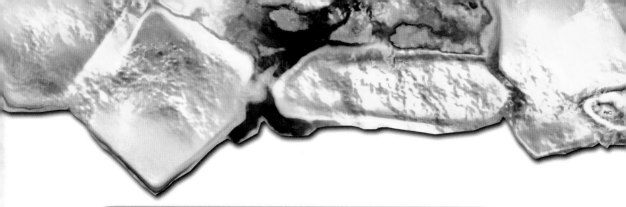

CAUSE:

American miners' distrust of immigrant miners grew.
They blamed the immigrant miners for their
problems in the mines.

EFFECTS:

- Immigrant miners were physically attacked by American miners.
- American miners accused immigrant miners of crimes they hadn't committed.
- A Foreign Miners Tax was placed on immigrant miners, charging them $20 per month for a miner's permit.

April 1850—The Foreign Miners Tax charges immigrants $20 a month to mine in California.

1852—Another tax requires immigrant miners to pay $3 a month.

March 14, 1851—The Foreign Miners Tax is repealed.

1852—Gold becomes harder to find in California.

After the Gold Rush

By the mid-1850s, many of California's formerly booming mining towns were empty. Some people had found their fortunes in the mines, but most found hard times and little reward. Some returned East to the homes they'd left behind. Others settled in California's larger cities such as San Francisco and Sacramento, where they started businesses. Others started farms in the country.

Much of the land where miners had searched for gold became productive farmland.

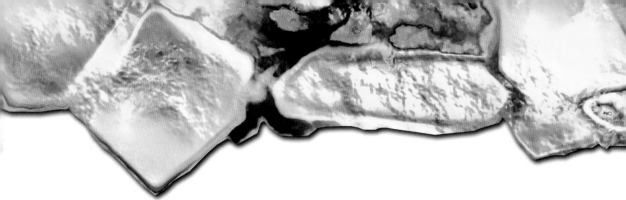

The gold rush was over, but it had changed California and the entire country. It opened up the West to hundreds of thousands of people and soon led to the first transcontinental railroad linking the East and West Coasts. After the American Civil War ended in 1865, thousands more Americans settled in California. Agriculture became one of California's most important businesses and remains so today. As more people moved to California, the state's population soared and other businesses prospered.

The gold rush brought people of different backgrounds and beliefs from around the world to settle in a new land where anything might be possible, even golden riches. Although most failed to become rich from gold, many people from around the world began new lives and found success in other ways. The California gold rush had changed the United States forever.

San Francisco's harbor

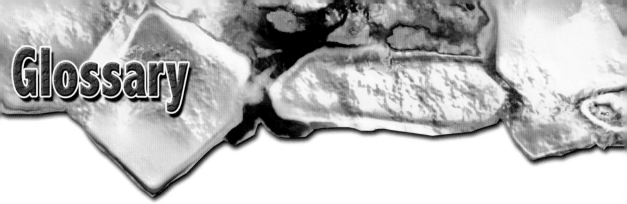

Glossary

annex (AA-nehks) To take over or add to.

discrimination (dihs-krih-muh-NAY-shun) The act of treating a person or group of people unfairly just because they are different.

frontier (fruhn-TIHR) The edge of a settled country where the wilderness begins.

immigrant (IH-muh-gruhnt) A person who comes from another country to live in a new country.

isthmus (IHSS-muhs) A narrow strip of land connecting two larger pieces of land.

migration (my-GRAY-shun) A movement from one place or country to another.

occupation (ah-kyuh-PAY-shun) The holding and control of an area by military force.

outpost (OWT-pohst) A frontier settlement.

prospector (PRAH-spehk-tuhr) A person who explores an area, usually looking for gold or another valuable element.

repeal (rih-PEEL) To put an official end to a law.

telegraph (TEH-luh-graf) A system for sending messages over an electric wire using coded signals.

transcontinental (tranz-kahn-tuh-NEHN-tuhl) Going across a continent.

tributary (TRIH-byuh-tehr-ee) A stream feeding into a larger stream, river, or lake.

Index

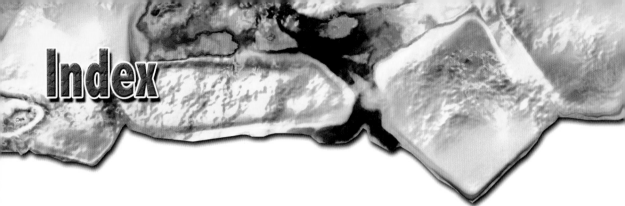